DICK
KING-SMITH'S
ANIMAL
FRIENDS

For Myrle
D. K.~S.

For Deirdre and Lucy
A. J.

Text copyright © 1996 by Foxbusters Ltd.
Illustrations copyright © 1996 by Anita Jeram

First U.S. edition 1996

Library of Congress Cataloging-in-Publication Data

King-Smith, Dick.
[Animal friends]
Dick King-Smith's animal friends / Dick King-Smith ;
illustrated by Anita Jeram. — 1st U.S. ed.
Summary: A collection of anecdotes about the author's encounters
with animals beginning with his first elephant ride at the zoo
and continuing through his years as a dairy farmer.
ISBN 1-56402-960-3
1. Animals — Anecdotes — Juvenile literature.
2. King-Smith, Dick — Juvenile literature.
[1. Animals — Anecdotes. 2. King-Smith, Dick.]
I. Jeram, Anita, ill. II. Title.
QL49.K55   1996
591 — dc20   95-51710

10 9 8 7 6 5 4 3 2 1

Printed in Hong Kong

This book was typeset in Cochin and the titles were
typeset in Bernhard Modern.
The pictures were done in watercolor and ink.

Candlewick Press
2067 Massachusetts Avenue
Cambridge, Massachusetts 02140

— DICK —
KING-SMITH'S
ANIMAL
FRIENDS

Thirty-one
True Life Stories

ILLUSTRATED BY
ANITA JERAM

CANDLEWICK PRESS
CAMBRIDGE, MASSACHUSETTS

Me, not so long ago, at a friend's farm.

me, age 2½, on our front lawn.

I THOUGHT I WOULD TELL YOU ABOUT SOME OF MY ANIMAL FRIENDS.

Ever since I was very little, I've enjoyed the company of animals, big and small. I can still remember the thrill of riding on an elephant at the zoo when I was four, and the excitement of getting my first white mice.

As a schoolboy, I was crazy about pets, and even

as a wartime soldier I kept chameleons in North Africa and a puppy in Italy.

In my new school uniform, age 9.

Still at school, age 17.

After the war came twenty years of farming. I was married by then, with three children, and we lived in the country surrounded by all sorts of beasts and birds.

Later, as the host of a children's TV show, I worked with tons of different creatures, from chickens to chimps, from pigs to pythons.

It's not surprising that I like to write stories about animals. This is a book of little tales about a few of my animal friends.

Age 36, with Monty, my pig.

Some I was very fond of and knew for their entire lives, like Dodo the dachshund or Frank the rabbit.

Some I had for only a very short time, like the golden pheasants.

And some, like the two badgers or Midnight the angry cow, weren't all that friendly to me!

But all were interesting—one way or another—and each was unforgettable. I've enjoyed writing about them.

If you enjoy reading about them,

then everyone's happy!

List *of* Stories

The Elephant Ride

I REMEMBER, WHEN I WAS QUITE YOUNG, GOING for a ride on an elephant at the zoo. I imagined that we were in the jungle, and a tiger would appear.

I would be quite safe, of course, on top of the elephant. All the same I think I was very glad to see my mother appear instead and wave to me.

No Luck

WHEN I WAS ABOUT EIGHT, I HAD a tortoise. I didn't know if it was male or female. By day it plodded around slowly on a patch of grass. At night I put an upturned wooden box over it to keep it warm and dry, to keep it from wandering off and getting lost, and to protect it from eagles. (There weren't any eagles where I lived, but I had seen a picture in a storybook of an eagle carrying off a tortoise.)

One morning I discovered that my tortoise was a she. I lifted up the wooden box and there beside her was a little round egg, like a Ping-Pong ball.

I didn't say anything to anyone about the tortoise egg, but took it into our house and upstairs to the linen closet, where sheets and pillowcases and blankets were all laid out, on wooden shelves in the warm darkness. I carefully put my egg between some nice thick blankets.

I wasn't sure how long it took for tortoise eggs to hatch, so I kept going to look at it, every day for ages and ages.

I didn't realize you had to have a father tortoise as well as a mother.

Tree Frog

ONCE, LONG AGO, I WAS given a green tree frog. All I can recall about it is that it was very small, bright green in color, and had suckers on the ends of its fingers and toes so that it could climb up a pane of glass.

Catching the Skipper

ONE OF MY GRANDFATHERS WAS a very enthusiastic lepidopterist: that's to say, someone who collects butterflies and moths. I don't think this happens so much nowadays. I hope not.

He had a beautifully made mahogany cabinet with dozens of slender drawers in it, each containing trays on which the bodies of hundreds of different butterflies and moths were carefully mounted, their wings spread, their colors as beautiful as they were in life.

SKIPPERS Hesperiidae ♂♂♂

He was a very kind and gentle man, my grandfather was. Yet somehow he never seemed disturbed by the thought of killing all those lovely insects. He caught each one in his butterfly net and then put it in what we called a "stink bottle," a jar filled with some poisonous stuff that killed it.

One day he took me with him to try to catch a small brown butterfly called a Lulworth Skipper, so named

LULWORTH

because it had first been discovered at Lulworth Cove in Dorset, England. At that time my grandfather had a car called a Clyno, a dignified sort of machine that didn't go very fast — especially when he was driving.

At twenty miles per hour it took an awfully long time to drive the hundred-odd miles to Lulworth. When we arrived at last and began to comb the steep sides of the cove, there was no sign of a Lulworth Skipper.

After a couple of hours, just as we were about to give up and start the long, slow journey home, up fluttered a small dingy brown butterfly.

Quickly my grandfather handed me the net (I was a good fifty years younger, so a lot faster than he was).

Off I dashed, swung the net,

and caught the Lulworth Skipper.

We came,

we saw,

we conquered!

A Palace Fit for Mice

I USED TO KEEP MASSES OF PET MICE.

Many of them I bought from a mouse farm in South Wales, where you could buy more than forty different kinds of mice.

I became a member of the National Mouse Club and I wore a little pin with a picture of a mouse under the letters N.M.C.

But what I liked best about owning mice was building cages for them. The cages I built were nothing less than mouse palaces. They were very big with glass fronts so that I could see my mice running around.

Inside there were two floors with stairs connecting them, and lots of little walkways and bridges so that the mice got plenty of exercise; and of course there were cozy sleeping boxes in the upstairs bedrooms, where the mother mice could have their children (and a great many children they had).

Some people find it restful to watch fish in a fish tank. What I liked best was watching mice in a mouse palace.

A Short Stay

WHEN I WAS ABOUT FIFTEEN OR SO, I WAS LUCKY enough to have a wonderful place to keep some of my pets. It was an unused grass tennis court that had been fenced around with chicken wire, sides and top, to make a huge cage. In it I kept lots of guinea pigs and rabbits, and a tortoise or two.

One unforgettable day I was given two new pets: a pair of golden pheasants. Like many female birds (who need to be camouflaged while they're sitting on their eggs), the hen golden pheasant is plainly colored, a yellowish brown striped with black.

But the cock golden pheasant is a magnificent-looking fellow, with a very long tail and brilliant feathers of gold and scarlet. On his head is a glowing yellow crest, and on his shoulders, a fiery amber cape, or ruff, above dark green patches. You can't imagine a more colorful bird. This one minced around his mate with little high-stepping strides, his ruff raised, and gave a shrill whistle.

You can imagine my feelings of delight when these pheasants — my pheasants — arrived that morning.

But you certainly can't imagine what I felt like later in the day. In the roof of the cage there was, unknown to anyone, a hole where the wire had rusted away. The golden pheasants found it.

That evening I went to feed them, and they were no longer there. The rabbits and the guinea pigs hopped and scurried around as usual, and the tortoises slow-marched around, but the pheasants were gone.

The hen bird had disappeared altogether, but the cock was sitting in the top of a tall tree nearby, his colors brilliant in the light of the setting sun. There was nothing I could do, no possible way of catching him.

I could only stand and stare. By the morning he was gone. I never saw him again.

More and More Rats

Nobody much likes rats. They are thought of as vicious, cunning, smelly carriers of disease. Pet rats, on the other hand, are very clean and easy to handle and make fascinating companions.

I know that the pair I once had couldn't have been more likable. They were Japanese Hooded rats, pure white on the sides and legs, with a black head and a black line down the back.

I called them Jupiter and Juno, after a Roman god and goddess. Jupiter was quite a bit bigger than Juno. He was very tame and liked to travel around sitting on my shoulder.

Juno was usually too busy for that sort of thing.

Busy?

Doing what?

Having babies.

In her first litter she had ten babies. In her second, twelve. In her third, sixteen.

What happened to all those young rats? I can't remember — it was so long ago.

But I do remember old Jupiter very clearly, perched on my shoulder, tickling my neck with his whiskers. He especially loved chocolate chip cookies.

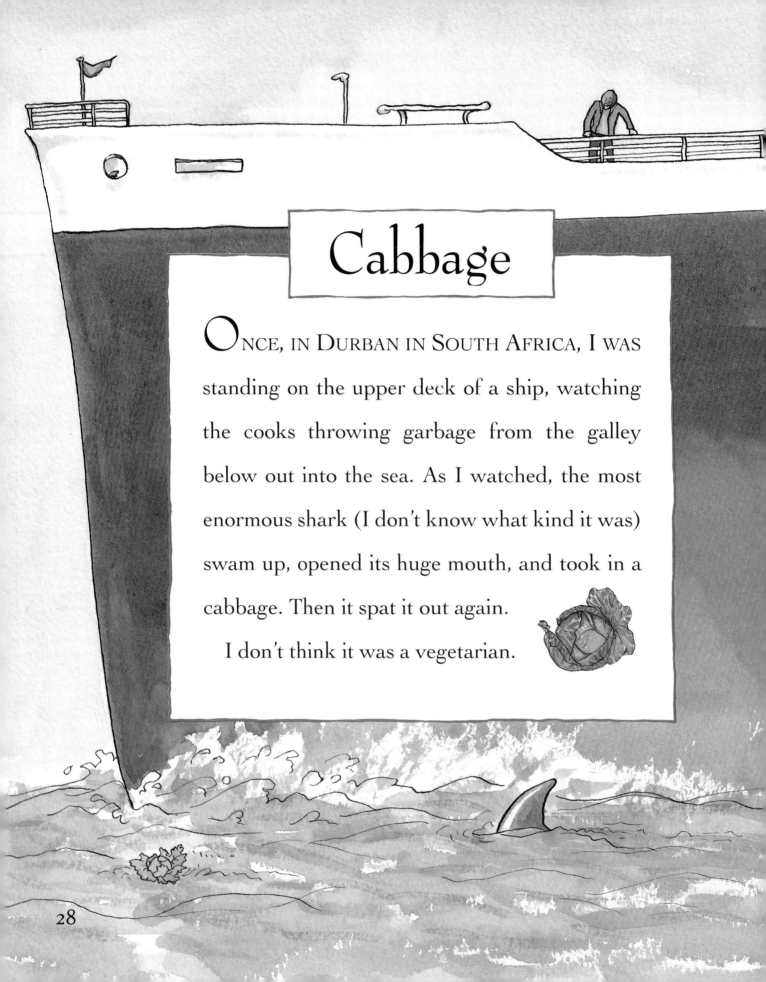

Cabbage

ONCE, IN DURBAN IN SOUTH AFRICA, I WAS standing on the upper deck of a ship, watching the cooks throwing garbage from the galley below out into the sea. As I watched, the most enormous shark (I don't know what kind it was) swam up, opened its huge mouth, and took in a cabbage. Then it spat it out again.

I don't think it was a vegetarian.

Chameleon Hunting

Being bitten by a chameleon is a funny feeling. It doesn't really hurt at all. It's more of a grip than a bite. It's as though someone is pinching your finger with a pair of pliers, but very gently.

Before a chameleon bites you, it threatens you with a gaping mouth, sometimes hissing and swaying angrily from side to side.

Once I had a big cardboard box full of chameleons, about twelve of them. I'd better explain, in case you think that's a cruel way to keep them.

It was during World War II and we were driving west along the top of Africa, from Cairo all the way to Tripoli. Every evening, when we stopped, I went chameleon hunting, and I soon filled my box.

I only kept them in the box while we were actually traveling. When we stopped, I took them all out and put them on a bush or a low tree branch so that they could catch flies and other insects, which is what they eat. Just in case they didn't have any luck, I swatted lots of flies and put them in the box.

There was no danger of losing my chameleons, because they moved so slowly.

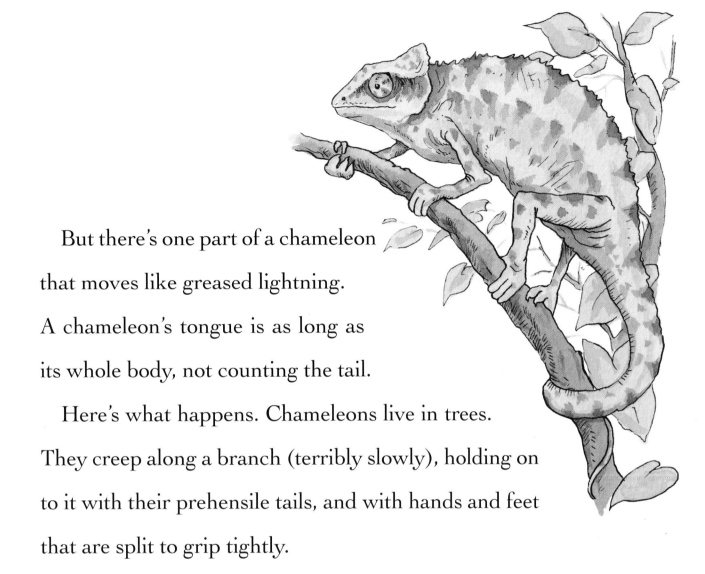

But there's one part of a chameleon
that moves like greased lightning.
A chameleon's tongue is as long as
its whole body, not counting the tail.

Here's what happens. Chameleons live in trees.
They creep along a branch (terribly slowly), holding on
to it with their prehensile tails, and with hands and feet
that are split to grip tightly.

Along comes a fly and settles, so it
thinks, well out of chameleon range.

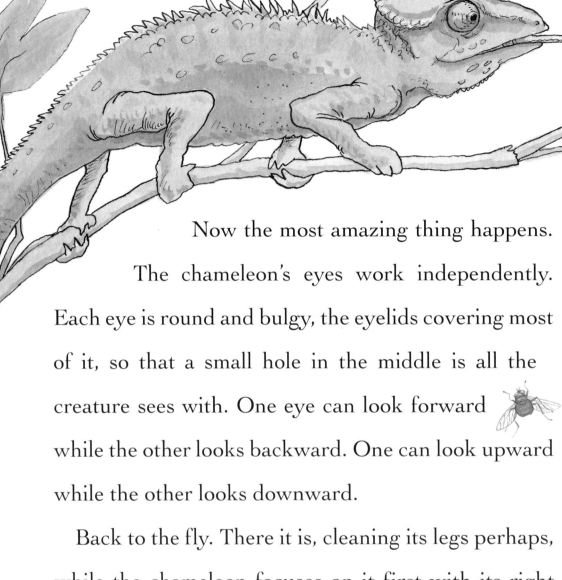

Now the most amazing thing happens. The chameleon's eyes work independently. Each eye is round and bulgy, the eyelids covering most of it, so that a small hole in the middle is all the creature sees with. One eye can look forward while the other looks backward. One can look upward while the other looks downward.

Back to the fly. There it is, cleaning its legs perhaps, while the chameleon focuses on it first with its right eye, then with its left. Then, from out of the blue, the entire length of that clubbed sticky tongue shoots out and it's good-bye fly.

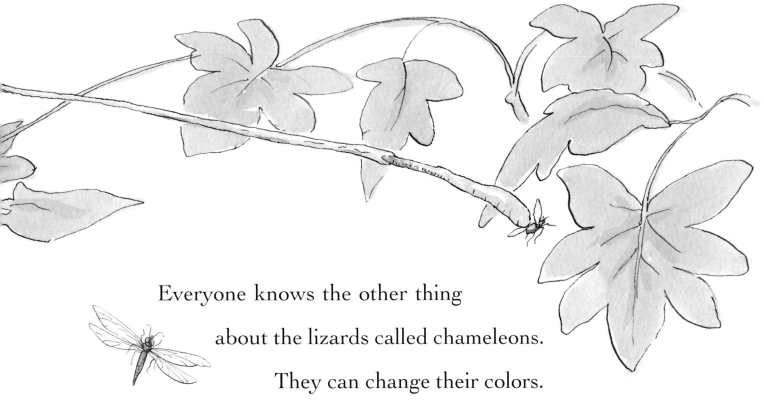

Everyone knows the other thing
about the lizards called chameleons.
They can change their colors.

My chameleons stayed mostly brownish if they were
in the cardboard box or sitting on the knees of my
uniform pants. On bushes they turned greenish, on
sand, yellowish.

At night they were usually cream colored
with yellow patches and when excited, they turned
a sort of reddish brown with golden spots. When
they were really angry, those golden spots turned
black.

I was fascinated by them and didn't mind how often they bit me. As time went by, they became used to me and treated me more kindly. Just before we got to Tripoli, I let them all go. I didn't think they'd enjoy coming on the invasion of Italy.

I sat watching them move away, very, very slowly, into the bushes, hands gripping, feet gripping, tails gripping, eyes swiveling. Somewhere inside each mouth a catapult tongue waited, coiled like a spring.

I watched till every last chameleon was gone from sight.

Killed on Active Duty

I HAVE HAD A GREAT NUMBER OF DOGS, many of whom lived to a good age. But one died young, killed on active duty.

It was 1943 and we were fighting our way up the mountainous west coast of Italy.

Somewhere in a hilltop village, I came across this puppy, for that's all she was, and bought her with a couple of packs of cigarettes.

She was a very Italian-looking puppy —
the color of milky coffee, a kind of
slender, long-tailed terrier.
I named her Vicky.

She traveled with us for several weeks, ate well, and
was much spoiled by everyone. Then I had an attack of
jaundice and had to go back to Naples, to the hospital.

When I got back to the battalion, they told me that
Vicky had been killed. She'd run across a road right
in front of a truck. I never saw her grave because
we'd moved on, but apparently they'd given
her a proper burial and a wooden
cross on which was written:

VICKY, GRENADIER GUARDS

Lazy Ben

I ONCE OWNED A BULL NAMED BEN. HE WAS AN Aberdeen Angus, which meant that like all his breed he was deep bodied, short legged, and hornless, with a shiny, satiny, coal black coat.

Ben was also very lazy. Now, you should never trust a bull — of any breed — but I don't think Ben would have hurt a fly. It would have been too much effort.

When Ben was in the cowshed, he wore a stout leather strap around his neck, like a giant dog collar, with a length of chain attached to it.

But one fine summer's morning, when the cows had gone out to graze and Ben was left alone in his stall, he managed to slip his head out of the collar. Whose fault it was I don't remember, but either I or my cowman, Francis, hadn't fastened it tight enough.

The cowshed had three doors and all of them were wide open, but Ben couldn't be bothered to walk as far as the nearest one.

He simply put his great head against the wooden outer wall of the old cowshed, and pushed.

I know because I was sweeping the yard and saw it.

In circuses they used to have dogs that were trained to jump through paper hoops, and that's what it looked like. With a loud splintering noise, first Ben's head and then his body came clean through the wall, with pieces of wood flying everywhere.

Very slowly, so as not to waste energy, Ben ambled into the nearest field and began to graze.

Before I could do anything, I heard a wild shout of anger, and Francis, arriving back from breakfast on his old bicycle, pedaled past me and out into the field.

Throwing down the bike, he ran after Ben, who, alarmed by the angry shouts, began to trot away and finally even broke into a lumbering canter.

Right across the skyline they ran as I watched; but the bull was fat and slow, and the cowman was lean and fast. He soon caught up with Ben.

The last I saw before they
disappeared behind a hedge

was Francis grabbing hold of the end of Ben's tail and

pulling it like a man in a tug of war.

I ran to help them but I wasn't needed. Ben was so

 tired out that he couldn't manage

more than the slowest of walks

behind Francis, who had one

finger (the little one) crooked

through the ring in the bull's nose.

We tied him up again, making sure the collar was tight

enough, and set about fixing the cowshed wall.

As for Ben, he gave a great sigh and

flopped down, all worn out.

Susie

Susie was a small, hairy black-and-white terrier. I got her from an old fellow named Jack when she was about the size of a guinea pig.

Later, she grew bigger than that, but not much.

Susie was always very short tempered, growling at anyone who said things like, "Get off my chair, Susie."

She loved me best but she growled at me just as much. She followed me everywhere.

If I was plowing, Susie would trot behind the plow in the newly turned furrow, up and down the field, all day long.

During her long life she had numerous brushes with death, but there's one I remember above all the others.

One December day — a bitterly cold day it was, with a biting east wind — Susie disappeared. The days passed with no sign of her, and my wife and I sadly resigned ourselves to the fact that at last her luck had run out.

Eight days later, as I came out of the back door of the farmhouse to start the morning milking, I saw a filthy, bedraggled little object dragging herself painfully up the yard.

We could only suppose she'd been stuck somewhere deep below ground and perhaps had to wait till she became thin enough to struggle free.

To have survived eight days and nights in freezing weather with nothing to eat was somewhat believable, but with nothing to drink? Impossible — for any dog except Susie.

We cleaned her up, fed her warm milk mixed with glucose and egg, and within a day she was her old self.

We couldn't have been more pleased to have her back, but if Susie was pleased too, she never showed it. She just growled at us and snarled at all the other dogs as usual.

Badger Bopping

I BET THERE AREN'T MANY
people who can say, "Once I bopped a
badger on the bottom with my hat."

I can. I was going out early one summer
morning to bring the cows in for milking.
On my way I had to cross a big pasture,
and there, right in the middle of it,
was a badger.

Now, badgers are nocturnal animals and, although there was a big burrow in the nearby woods, where we often heard them clucking and chattering at night, it wasn't often that we saw them in broad daylight.

So I hurried toward this solitary badger, hoping that it wouldn't run away till I'd had a good look at it. It didn't run away. It didn't take the slightest notice of me, even though I was now standing right beside it. It just continued snuffling around in the grass.

I felt rather foolish. I took off my hat and bopped the badger gently on its bottom.

It didn't even look up. "What's up with you, my friend?" I said. "Are you deaf, or blind, or both?"

Slowly, with that rolling bear-like shuffle that badgers have, it began to move toward the woods, while I continued to beat a light tattoo on its backside. At last it came to a hole in the hedge, and disappeared.

The very next morning I went exactly the same way to get the dairy herd, and there, in exactly the same place, were two badgers. My friend, I thought, and his friend!

Happily I ran toward them. With a volley of furious grunts, the two badgers charged at me. I fled at top speed.

Nobody ever believes this story.

But it's true.

Three Special Cats

DULCIE MAUDE

Our first special cat was a tortoiseshell-and-white queen called Dulcie Maude, who had, in her lifetime, one hundred and four kittens.

What's more, she liked to have them in unusual places such as a hay-filled manger in the stables or, on one occasion, in a large cardboard box half full of light bulbs.

The most comfortable place that Dulcie Maude ever chose was in a loft where lots of unwanted old toys were stored. One of these was a doll's carriage that still had its little pillow, blue blankets, and pink quilt in it.

The doll had long disappeared, but in its place Dulcie Maude lay purring happily in the carriage, nursing yet another brood of children.

HIGH JINKS

THE SECOND SPECIAL CAT I remember was a ginger-colored female by the name of Jinks. Jinks lived to be very old — I can't remember how many kittens she had. But I do remember that I first brought her home as a kitten herself. She'd been born in a warehouse and she was really quite wild, so before I took her out of the box I'd carried her home in, I made sure that the room we were in was escape proof. I shut the door, closed all the windows, and let Jinks out of the box.

Luckily, it was summer and there was no fire in the grate, because the kitten dashed straight up the chimney.

What wasn't so lucky was that the chimney needed sweeping, and down came an avalanche of soot. By the time I'd managed to reach up inside the chimney and grab hold of the kitten, I was covered in the stuff.

As for Jinks, she had changed color completely, from ginger to coal black.

LOVING LUPIN

THE THIRD OF MY SPECIAL CATS WAS ANOTHER ginger — long haired this time and a tom. His name was Lupin and in fact he belonged to one of our daughters. But when she and her family went to live in America for a year, Lupin came to stay with us.

Lupin was special because he was in some ways more dog than cat. He bossed our dogs around, and when we took them for walks, Lupin would come too, marching along behind, waving his plumy tail.

And there was another way in which he was different.

Most cats like to keep to themselves, accepting admiration and affection from their owners, but not giving much back. Lupin was very loving. He would rub his big round furry face against ours, purring like a steam engine and making quite a fuss over us.

But we were only the cat sitters. When his real owner came back after that year in America, you should have seen the fuss that Lupin made over her.

Talk about true love!

Nanny Anna

P<small>EOPLE THINK THAT A DACHSHUND IS JUST A KIND</small> of short-legged, long-bodied dog. They do not realize that there are dogs . . . and there are dachshunds.

Dogs like to please their owners by doing what they are told. Dachshunds like to please themselves.

Our first dachshund was a wire-haired one. We named her Anna. When we got her as a puppy, she took not the slightest notice of anything we said to her.

"She must be stone deaf," we said.

But she wasn't. She was just a dachshund.

Apart from being as stubborn as all her breed, Anna's specialty was mother love. Quite early in her life we began to call her Nanny.

She did not need to be nursing her own puppies — she would nurse anything. Kittens were well received if there was a cat crisis. And once she tried to play mother to four piglets that a young sow had rejected. Nanny thought that they were lovely and immediately settled down to nurse them in her basket.

Alas, newborn piglets, unlike puppies, have sharp little teeth, but still Anna put up with them till they could be fostered on to another sow.

She saved their lives, in fact.

The Pig Harness

THE FIRST PIG I EVER OWNED WAS A PEDIGREE Yorkshire named Molly. Molly was not only beautiful and intelligent (as all pigs are), but also very sensible and easygoing.

At that time I had only one old pigpen, and I didn't like to see her confined in it — I wanted her to have more freedom. Equally, I didn't want to spend a lot of money on fencing. Looking in a farming magazine, I found the solution: a "pig harness."

I sent away for it.

The harness consisted of stout leather straps that buckled around the pig's body, and were then attached to a length of chain that looked strong enough to anchor the *QE2*.

The chain ended in a huge expanding spring, and the spring was fixed to a large steel spike that was driven deep into the ground with a sledgehammer.

Once harnessed, the pig could then move freely in a large circle around the spike, but no farther. With help, I buckled the straps around Molly's large white body.

She stood patiently for the fitting, her attention held by a trough full of food.

Then the harness was
attached to the chain that
was attached to the spike.

Her food finished, Molly moved away slowly in her
new outfit, until at last she reached the limit of the
chain and came to a full stop. She grunted and
strained against this mysterious thing that was
holding her back.

"No use trying to

bust that, old girl," I said.

"That spike and that spring and
that chain would hold an elephant."

Molly's reply was a loud squeal of anger.

Then she pulled with all her strength
against the pig harness.

The spike held firm.

The spring,

now fully expanded,

held. The chain held.

But suddenly all the stout leather

straps and buckles burst apart,

and Molly trotted

happily away.

Midnight

I ONCE BOUGHT A BLACK COW, THE BLACKEST COW you ever saw, coal black, raven black, as black as midnight (which is what I called her).

Sharp and curved were Midnight's horns, and seeing her in the sale ring I was reminded of pictures of the fighting bulls of Spain.

For some strange reason she went very cheap, and I was pleased with my bargain when they delivered her in time for the afternoon milking.

What a milking that was.

At the first touch of the first milking cup on the first teat, Midnight exploded into a burst of kicking that stripped the machine into its component parts and left me battered, bruised, and breathless.

The sheer ferocity of the animal was frightening: she leaped and pranced and bawled in anger. Her fierce eyes blazed and there was no doubt about what she would have done with those twin daggers on her head if the neck chain hadn't restrained her.

A few days later she charged my wife, who escaped under a fence in a great hurry.

"What happened?" I said.

"She put her head down and started to paw at the ground, and then she gave a horrible kind of roar and came straight for me."

"She'll have to go," I said.

She went.

63

Tortoise Riding

Lots of people, including me, can say they've fallen off a horse at some time or another. But how many can say (as I can), "I've fallen off a tortoise"?

It was, of course, a giant tortoise.

Most giant tortoises live in the Galápagos Islands, in the Pacific. Actually, the tortoise I was riding was not from the Galápagos, but from an island in the Indian Ocean called Aldabra.

I'm not sure which tortoise is the bigger – the Aldabra
or the Galápagos – but this one was certainly big enough.
I sat astride its huge shiny shell and said, "Gee-up!"
Nothing happened.

Then with a sudden lurch,

the tortoise took a large step forward.

I fell off backward and landed

on my bottom with a bump.

Alas, Poor Evil

MY BROTHER ONCE HAD A FERRET named Evil. Evil was a hob (a male ferret); his long snaky body was a dirty yellow color, his eyes pink. Despite his name, he was quite good-natured with people he knew.

But one fine day, Evil somehow escaped from his cage and disappeared. We sent out a search party, but there was no sign of the ferret.

Later, a friend of my brother's named Jeff was rummaging around in the shed, looking for something or other, when, under a pile of old trash, he found Evil, and grabbed hold of him.

Evil was not very pleased.

He bit deep into Jeff's thumb.

That evening (the ferret now safely back in his cage), Jeff went to his doctor for a tetanus shot. His mind was full of thoughts of blood poisoning or even rabies, which would lead to a painful death.

In fact he suffered no ill effects.

But that night Evil died.

Goats on the Bed

I USED TO KNOW SOME PEOPLE WHO KEPT A lot of goats. They lived in a bungalow (the people, I mean, not the goats).

One day, on my way to visit these people in their yard, I walked past their bedroom window and happened to look in. There, lying happily on the bed, chewing their cud, were two large nanny goats.

I mentioned this to the people.

"Oh, no!" they said. "Crumbs in the bed are bad enough, but goat droppings are ridiculous!"

Tree Fox

Not far from the cottage where we live now is a long, narrow thicket beside a small stream.

My wife and I were walking along the edge of it one late September morning when we saw a fox — a male fox by the size of him — slip into the far end of the thicket.

When we passed through the same gap, we were surprised to see no sign of him. Although our three dachshunds — Dodo, Poppy, and Little Elsie — marked his trail eagerly, they lost the scent and interest after a little ways.

This scene was replayed on several walks,

and always the dogs lost the scent at the

same place, beneath a big old crack willow.

As such trees often do, it leaned out over the stream,

its thick trunk at a forty-five-degree angle

to the ground.

We never found a burrow in the thicket, so always

presumed that the fox, on hearing or scenting us,

simply slid out on the far side and ran away.

Until one day, standing beneath the willow,

we happened to look upward.

There he sat on a comfortable branch

fifteen feet up, paws together, tail

curled neatly around him, ears pricked,

looking down on us.

What a patronizing look it was.

We left, feeling small.

Walking Frank

I'VE OWNED DOZENS AND DOZENS OF rabbits — many different breeds — but Frank is the one I'll always remember. He was a French lop, a very big kind of rabbit with drooping ears. In color he was what's known in England as a butterfly smut — whitish, with lots of brown spots and patches, and on the muzzle a butterfly-shaped marking.

At the time I also had a number of Dutch does, small black-and-white rabbits, and Frank became the father of the oddest collection of children.

Some were black and white, some brown and white, some had smudges on their nose, some didn't. Some had sticking-up ears, some had hanging-down ears, and some had one ear up and one ear down.

Frank loved his food. I weighed him once when he was in his prime and he tipped the scales at eighteen pounds. He was so big that I nailed three hutches together so that he wouldn't feel cramped.

I used to exercise
him too, on a collar
and leash. Frank liked
these walks. Often he'd
suddenly do a great buckjump

in the air to show his pleasure. The problem was that
whereas taking a dog for a walk means that the dog
goes wherever you want, taking a rabbit for a walk
means going wherever the rabbit wants.

And Frank always chose the vegetable garden.

Leslie

As we were driving home one night, our car headlights discovered a hedgehog in the middle of the road. The lights and the sound of the approaching car had caused it to roll up into a ball.

Hedgehogs have it firmly in their minds that if they're rolled up, they're safe. They may be safe from some predators, but not from cars or trucks.

I picked up this hedgehog in an old rag, and we took him home. Or we took her home; we couldn't tell. So we named him or her Leslie, a name that suits a boy or a girl.

Leslie spent that night in a spare rabbit hutch, and by the next morning was quite ready to have a good drink and a meal of canned dog food, which hedgehogs like very much.

For several days we kept him or her, hoping that if he or she got used to us, he or she might stay when we released him or her into our garden. Hedgehogs are very useful in gardens because they eat slugs and snails.

One evening we gave Leslie a last good meal, then put him or her down on the lawn, and watched as he or she trotted away. Ours is a walled garden. What we didn't know then was that hedgehogs are good at climbing walls.

We never saw Leslie again.

Bribery

I WAS ONCE ALLOWED TO HOLD A BABY FEMALE chimpanzee in a safari park. I sat on a bench, and she sat on my knee, put her arms around my neck, and gave me some rubbery kisses.

We were getting along really well together until the little chimp spotted Dodo, my miniature red wire-haired dachshund, who was underneath the bench. The chimp reached down a long arm, and I could see her thinking, "I'm going to pull that dog's hair."

Dodo flinched, and I could see her thinking, "That creature is going to pull my hair."

The chimp pulled Dodo's hair.

Luckily I had come prepared for naughty behavior. I took a roll of mints out of my pocket and the chimpanzee instantly forgot all about the dog. She took a mint from me, delicately between thumb and forefinger, popped it into her mouth, crunched, swallowed, and held out her hand politely for more.

How I would have loved to take her home with me.

How unhappy Dodo would have been.

Eric

Once I carried an Indian python, draped around my neck, for almost half an hour. His name was Eric.

Eric was not a really big python. At his widest part he was about as thick as a man's thigh, and he was around ten feet in length. Some pythons can be more than twice as long as this.

Some people think that snakes are cold and slimy. Eric's skin was warm and dry, and it was easy to feel the power of the thousands of muscles in his beautifully marked body.

I wore him around my neck and shoulders like a giant scarf, and he was heavy, I can tell you. But he behaved perfectly, and I didn't feel the least bit nervous of him.

Except perhaps toward the end of our meeting, when Eric began to feel he'd had enough.

At least I think that's what he was trying to say when he started to squeeze my neck, just a little. I handed him back to his keeper.

The Hitchhiker

We were once driving to west Wales, at the start of a family vacation at the seashore, when we saw something very small and yellow waddling along the middle of the road in front of us.

It was a duckling.

It was quite alone and appeared determined to go to the ocean, too. So we gave it a ride and some chocolate cake. And afterward we brought it home.

Solomon and Albert

I ONCE KNEW A LLAMA THAT HATED a zebra. Or was it a zebra that hated a llama? I'm not sure. All I know is that they were not the best of friends.

They lived in adjoining pastures, separated by a high chainlink fence. On one side was Albert the llama, and on the other side was Solomon the zebra. Every day they would put on the same performance, just like actors in a long-running play.

First, Albert would come up to the wire and stick his head over it, and he would stare at Solomon with that sneering, toothy, condescending stare that llamas have.

Solomon would notice of course, although he pretended not to. All the time he'd be grazing his way gradually over toward Albert.

Eventually Solomon would come close enough for Albert to do what he'd been wanting to do.

Angry llamas have a nasty habit of spitting at those they do not like, and when Albert judged Solomon to be near enough, he would spit at him.

At precisely the same instant, Solomon, with a shrill neigh of fury, would whip around and lash out at Albert with his hind hooves, trying to catch him on the chin. I never saw either of them score — it was always a draw. Solomon's heels never quite reached Albert, and Albert's spit never quite hit Solomon.

But each lived in hope that one day he'd succeed.

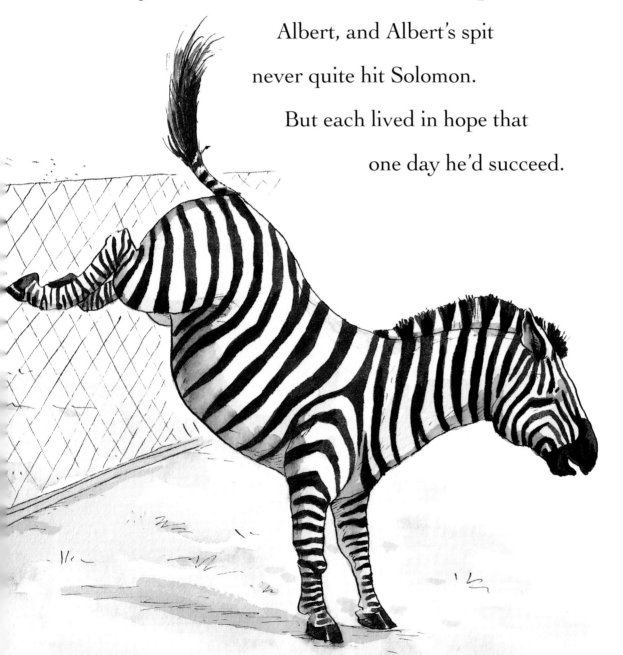

The Stowaway

O<small>N A CRUISE MY WIFE AND</small> I <small>TOOK TO THE</small> W<small>EST</small> Indies, there were about thirteen hundred people — passengers and crew — aboard the ship, and one pigeon.

It was a perfectly ordinary-looking pigeon, bluish gray and pink-legged, just like any one of the thousands of birds you see in city streets and squares.

But this was a very clever pigeon.

In no time at all it found out that not only do people on cruise liners eat a lot — they also spill and drop a lot of food on the deck.

The pigeon made itself at home on the promenade deck, where many of the passengers went to sit outside for breakfast and lunch. Every day, throughout these mealtimes, it strutted around underneath the tables, pecking up bits of food that had been dropped, sometimes maybe on purpose. Some thoughtful person always put down an ashtray filled with fresh water.

All the way across the Atlantic, the pigeon ate and ate, until it couldn't stand, but lay on its stomach.

Eventually, after weeks of feasting, it was put ashore.

But I wouldn't mind betting that it stowed away again on the very next cruise liner that stopped there.

Dodo: Star of the Show

OUR MINIATURE RED WIRE-HAIRED DACHSHUND, Dodo, was born on a farm in west Wales, and from the moment we picked her up to bring her home with us, it was plain that she was a most unusual dog.

Although young and small, she was very self-possessed. The first of our animals that she met was a Great Dane. He bent his huge head to this midget. She looked up and wagged her tail at him.

Some years later, when Dodo was about five, something happened that changed her life.

A television producer was looking for someone to host a small segment of a children's program. She needed someone who had been a farmer and a teacher and wrote books for children (that turned out to be me), and who also owned a small, attractive dog (that was Dodo).

Dodo and I must have made about fifty little films.

Although I improved as time went on, Dodo didn't need to: she was immediately at home in front of the cameras.

Not only did she like people, so she always got along very well with the film crews, she was also always extremely likeable herself.

At first the crew often came to our cottage; we filmed a number of animals there or nearby, and the crew always arrived promptly at nine o'clock on a Thursday morning.

By a quarter to nine each Thursday (and only on Thursdays), Dodo would be waiting by the door for them to arrive and admire her.

Don't ask me how she knew. I don't know.

After a while Dodo began to be recognized in public. In London once, I suddenly heard some children shout, "Look! It's Dodo!" and they rushed up and made a fuss over her, which she loved — not because she was vain, but because she was always so friendly to everyone.

And it wasn't only children who recognized her.

A train conductor once came to

punch my ticket (and hers).

"Why," he said, "if it isn't Dodo!"

She was always the star of the show.

Joe Crow

THE LATEST ANIMAL IN MY LIFE IS SITTING on the wall below my study window as I write. Now and again he looks up with a bright, considering eye. He is a young crow, just fledged. We call him Joe.

I first met Joe a week ago. He was hopping down the road. "Can't you fly?" I said, and for an answer he did, not very well, but well enough to get up onto my garden wall. A couple of hours later he was outside the back door, flapping his wings and opening his beak in a gesture that said plainly, "Feed me! Feed me!" Where his mother and father were, I don't know, but it was clear that I was expected to take their place. Now Joe is always waiting

for pieces of soaked dog food.

I feed them to him beside the greenhouse.

After he's eaten, Joe goes up to the side of
the greenhouse, sees another Joe reflected
in the window, and pecks angrily at it.

He's growing stronger and flying better every day.
This is not surprising really, because our friends who
live on the other side of the road (a hundred yards as the
crow flies) tell me that they are busy feeding a young
crow who keeps asking for food. And our next-door
neighbors say the same. Joe is no fool.

But we think of him as ours because he spends each
evening with us. We sit out in
the yard talking, and Joe sits on
the fence behind us with his head
to one side, listening. And at
night he roosts on our roof.

Postscript

R<small>EMEMBER</small> D<small>ODO</small>, <small>THE STAR OF THE</small> show? It might be nice, I'm thinking now, to end with a mention of another miniature red wire-haired dachshund named Little Elsie, who is sitting watching me.

Why? Because Little Elsie is Dodo's granddaughter.

She's a much different character from her granny — not as jolly and outgoing, less sure of herself (although she's as fierce as a lion when left in charge of the car) — in fact not the film star type.

But the older Little Elsie grows — and she's really quite old now, though still very active — the more she looks like her grandmother. Her red coat has paled with age, her beard and mustache are fuller, her muzzle is gray.

And lately a funny thing has begun to happen. We keep calling Elsie by the wrong name. Several times a day, one of us will say, "Come along, Dodo," and along comes Little Elsie, wagging her tail and doing her special trick, which is to bare her teeth in a grin of pleasure.